D0504247

invent it!

THE WORLD'S NEXT GREAT INVENTION IS INSIDE THIS BOOK ... JUST ADD YOU

ROB BEATTIE

QED

BRENT LIBRARIES

91120000331214	
Askews & Holts	28-Jun-2017
J600	£9.99

For Michael and Richard — the Collinson boys.

Q Quarto Knows

Quarto is the authority on a wide range of topics.
Quarto educates, entertains and enriches the lives of our readers—enthusiasts and lovers of hands-on living.
www.quartoknows.com

Copyright © 2017 Marshall Editions
First published in the UK in hardback in 2017
by QED Publishing
Part of The Quarto Group
The Old Brewery
6 Blundell Street
London N7 9BH

All rights reserved. No part of this publication may be reproduced, stored in a retrieval system, or transmitted in any form or by any means, electronic, mechanical, photocopying, recording, or otherwise, without the prior permission of the publisher, nor be otherwise circulated in any form of binding or cover other than that in which it is published and without a similar condition being imposed on the subsequent purchaser.

Illustrator: Apple Illustration Agency
Editorial Director: Laura Knowles
Art Director: Susi Martin
Publisher: Maxime Boucknooghe
Designed and edited by Tall Tree Ltd

ISBN: 978-1-78493-786-7

Printed and bound in China by Toppan Leefung

10 9 8 7 6 5 4 3 2 1   16 17 18 19 20

PICTURE CREDITS

(t=top, b=bottom, l=left, r=right, c=centre fc=front cover)

All images are public domain unless otherwise indicated.

Dreamstime.com: 6 (bl) Gorodok495, 7 (tl) Shotsstudio, 7 (cl) Kosmos111, 7 (tc) Shotsstudio, 7 (br) Dphiman, 7 (tr) Eastphoto, 12 (r) Liligraphie, 13 (br) Choneschones, 14 (cl) (c) Papound, 18 (bc) (c) Rvlsoft, 18 (br) Seregam, 20 (bl) Bear66, 20-21 (tc) Renzzo, 20-21 (c) Mikebraune, 20 (br) Sebalos, 21 (b) 22 (bl) 26 (bl) Kazzpix, 21 (br) Libux77, 22 (c) Raytags, 22-23 (c) Sergey Rudavin, 23 (bl) Sebalos, 22 (tr) Seregam, 24 (cl) Dule964, 24 (bl) Akiyoko74, 24 (bc) Gorodok495, 24 (r) Dphiman, 26 (cl) Taesmileland, 26 (l) Shaday365, 26 (cl) Plasticrobot, 26 (bc) Andre Bonn, 26 (cr) Annachizhova, 26 (br) Schankz, 27 (tl) Gavran333, 27 (b) Dphiman, 28 (l) Coprid, 29 (b)Zuperpups, 30 (bl) Vankad, 31 (cr) Porpeller, 33 (l) Sirawitmarch, 36 (r) Cmckna, 37 (tl) Georgios, 38 (bl) Cowardlion, 38 (bc) Miflippo, 38 (br) Nerthuz, 39 (bl) Jlvdream, 39 (br) Savcoco, 40 (bl) Kitch, 48 (tr) Arvinshen, 50 (bl) Iwka, 50 (c) Schankz, 50 (t) Shotsstudio, 50 (bc) Plasticrobot, 50 (br) Alexavich, 51 (tl) Zts, 51 (bl) Pioneer111, 51 (br) Xtremepixel, 56-57 (c) Albund, 58 (cl) Zkruger, 58 (b) Eastphoto

istockphoto.com: 4 (cl) CSA-Printstock, 10 (cl) ilbusca, 10-11 (c) Classix, 11 (tr) ilbusca, 15 (br) ivan-96, 16 (tr) ilbusca, 29 (t) ianlangley, 31 (tl) nicoolay, 33 (tr) Classix, 35 (br) Classix, 36 (l) ilbusca, 37 (b) Gosphotodesign, 39 (bc) Michaklootwijk, 41 (br) Classix, 42 (cr) ivan-96, 46 (t) robynmac, 46 (cr) kreinick, 53 (b) vgajic, 54 (l) spectrelabs, 59 (tr) Grafissimo, 59 (br) CSA-Prinstock, 60 (cl) CSA-Printstock, 60 (cr) CSA-Printstock, 62 (tl) nicoolay, 62 (l) Nikola Nastasic, 62 (bl) nicoolay

Shutterstock: 1 (c) practicuum, 6 (bc) 18 (bl) 19 (br) 25 (r) 34 (r) 41 (tl) 59 (c) Picsfive, 14 (tl - pen) Marek R. Swadzba, 17 (cr) Sign N Symbol Production, 18 (c) tsaplia, 19 (tr) Taigi, 27 (tc) optimarc, 43 (tr) Sign N Symbol Production, 57 (tr) Kostsov

CONTENTS

LET'S INVENT

Welcome to the wonderful world of inventions. Pop your pencil behind your ear, sit down and take the weight off your feet. There'll be plenty for you to do soon enough, so for now just relax and get to know your new surroundings.

WHAT TO EXPECT

If you're looking for a book that's going to do the hard work for you – maybe even come up with inventions for you to make – then you've come to the wrong place and you should just put this straight back on the shelf and move along.

* Roller skates for cats
* Wi-fi cheese grater
* Ham shoes
* Heat-seeking slippers
* Stealth tin opener
* Spring-loaded football boots

*INVENT-A-TRON 9000

ROUTE MAP

If you're still reading this, then you've taken the first steps on the journey to making your ideas a reality. This book will be your guide through the maze of inventing. It will ask you to make your own decisions – perhaps even go down a dead end or two – before arriving at your destination.

The Maze of Inventing

Reality
Almost There Avenue
Dead End
Marketing Mall
Dead End
Research Road
Prototype Place
Good Start Street
Idea

What we won't be doing is coming up with ideas for you. This kind of thing works best if you come up with the ideas yourself and are inspired to turn them into reality. We'll provide you with many of the mental tools, and plenty of hands-on suggestions, but all of the hard work is down to you.

COME ON THEN, THESE THINGS AREN'T GOING TO INVENT THEMSELVES!

INSPIRATIONAL INVENTORS

'Human inventions march from the complex to the simple, and simplicity is always perfection.'
Alexandre Dumas

'Our greatest weakness lies in giving up. The most certain way to succeed is always to try just one more time.'
Thomas Edison

'Logic will get you from A to Z. Imagination will get you everywhere.'
Albert Einstein

'Necessity is the mother of invention.'
Traditional proverb

THE INVENTION PROCESS

So you can see how the whole invention thing works from start to finish, we've put together this handy flowchart, which walks you through the steps required to turn a great idea into an amazing invention.

THINK IT!

At this stage, your invention is just a twinkle in your eye, a few sparks in your brain and an itch at the end of your fingers.

RESEARCH IT!

Time to look a little deeper and see whether the invention will work and if anyone will buy it and use it.

DESIGN IT!

So people like the idea, they think it'll work and it's never been done before – how can you make it attractive and useful so everybody really, really wants one?

BUILD IT!

This is where it gets really tricky. It's a great idea, people like it, you know they'll buy it... but can you actually make a prototype?

TEST IT!

Many inventions never reach the shops because they fail when put out into the real world. Now's the time to test yours to see if it passes or flunks.

PRODUCE IT!

It's time to get your invention made. You might be able to build it yourself, but, hopefully, it's going to be so successful that you'll need to get it mass-produced by the thousand!

PACKAGE IT!

The final piece of the puzzle – adding those little cosmetic touches and sprinkling some fairy dust over the top so that your finished invention says 'buy me!'.

PATENT IT!

Before your invention is ready to be released into the world, you must protect it legally from people who might love it so much that they want to steal the idea for themselves.

IMPROVE IT!

Even a great invention may need to be tweaked and refined a bit once it's been tested, so here's where you make little adjustments based on your feedback.

THINK IT!

When a cartoon character needs an idea, all they do is scrunch up their forehead, squeeze their eyes shut and wait for a light bulb to appear over their head. In real life, coming up with a great idea isn't so easy, but without one you'll never become a proper inventor.

THE CREATIVE KICKSTART

Here are some tried and tested ways to get the creative juices flowing:

TRY THIS...

Divide a piece of paper into columns. Then at the top of each one write down something you love to do – fishing, football, hanging out with your friends – and then come up with inventions to make them even better.

...OR THIS

Do the opposite. Make a list of the things you hate and then think of ways to stop them driving you crazy.

Let's PLAN

Deep Thoughts

ehh?

useless info

File it all HERE

The Secret Recipe

If there's a single, secret recipe for cooking up a great idea, it's this: don't just dream about things – do them. Great ideas are 1 per cent inspiration and 99 per cent perspiration, and that means you have to keep thinking of new ideas all the time until you come up with that killer invention.

Tools of the trade

The best inventors always have a sure-fire way to remember their greatest ideas, so make sure you always carry a notebook and pencil, or a smartphone to record your ideas or take photos of things that inspire you.

CREATIVE STUFF

GREAT Ideas!

...OR THIS

Do something repetitive that you don't have to think about, like shuffling a deck of cards; this frees up your mind to daydream.

...STILL STUCK

Flip through a dictionary, stop at random and write down the first word you see. Repeat 10 times. Putting random words together like this can inspire truly unique ideas.

F

...FINALLY

Do something physical. Exercise is like brain food and improves your ability to make connections and learn. It also makes you feel relaxed and happy, creating the perfect conditions for producing great ideas.

THINK ROUND CORNERS

When the techniques for coming up with a great idea on the previous pages don't work, try these wackier alternatives.

1. GO WINDOW SHOPPING

Look in a shop window and find an object there – any object. Move to the next shop window and find another object. Think of ways they could be used together. Headphones built into the hood of a jacket perhaps, or ice cream-flavoured paint.

How about combining an armchair with a ladder to make a piece of furniture you can escape from?

Not every alternative idea ends up being a success.

2. THINK BAD

Come up with a really terrible idea. Really, the worst idea you can think of. Then try to think of its opposite.

BLOW ON
THE GO!

Could you come up with an even worse idea than a tissue dispenser you wear on your head?

Are my ideas any good?

At this stage, the best way to know is to try them out on people who might use them – your target audience. They'll give you an honest answer, whereas your parents might want to encourage you (even if the idea is bad) and your friends might want to mess about. So don't try out your idea for a snazzy skateboard accessory on Grandad or that fantastic new knitting pattern delivery system on your big brother. If people aren't interested in your invention, they're more likely to be negative about what you're trying to do.

3. PEOPLE WATCH

Go out for a walk and look for things that frustrate people - parking, queuing for coffee, not being able to decide where to eat, being somewhere that's too noisy, being on their own - and think of ways to solve the problem.

This peddle-powered motorbike will help people to avoid the traffic.

4. IF I WERE...

Use the 'If I were...' approach. Imagine you're a famous footballer or musician or comedian and ask yourself how they would approach a particular problem.

OOPS!

5. FOCUS

Don't use the Internet or watch TV until you get a good idea. Now there's an incentive for you!

Invention Win

VELCRO

You'll find Velcro being used somewhere in every home, and even in outer space! It got its name by combining the French words for VELour (or velvet) and CROchet (or hook).

RESEARCH IT!

So you've come up with something you think will make a head-turning invention. Now you need to dig a little deeper to make sure your brilliant idea really is a brilliant idea!

HONEST ANSWERS, PLEASE

Here's a handy checklist that will help you to judge your invention idea objectively – with your head instead of your heart. Just make sure to give an honest answer to each question.

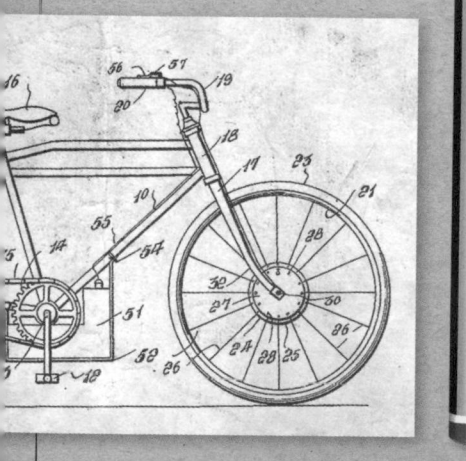

☐ 1. Is your idea actually new?

☐ 2. Would you pay good money for it?

☐ 3. Is your idea practical?

☐ 4. Is it simple to make?

☐ 5. Is it simple to explain?

☐ 6. Is your idea safe?

☐ 7. Can your idea be turned into a real invention?

☐ 8. Will other people find your invention useful?

☐ 9. Will people be able to afford your invention?

☐ 10. Does your invention have a 'WOW' factor?

If you can answer 'yes' to all 10 of these questions, you should go straight to page 18 and start designing your wonder-product, because you clearly don't need any more help from us! Any score below 6 out of 10 and you probably need to work on your idea a bit more.

5 26 27 28 29 30 cm

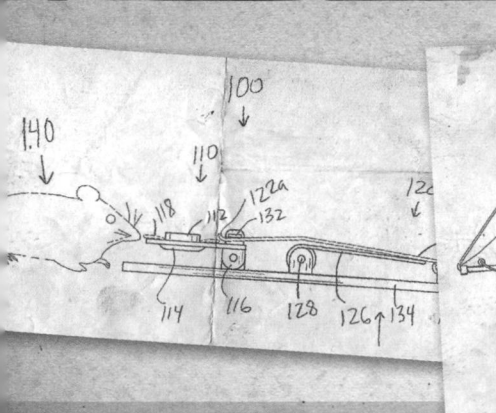

STOP, THIEF!

Before you go any further, make sure someone else hasn't already 'stolen' your brilliant idea – by coming up with it first. You can do this by checking the European Patent Office online. The website is a bit old-fashioned and some of the entries are long and complicated, but if someone else has already had the same idea and registered it, then you need to think again (we've got plenty more on patents and why they're important on pages 44–47).

To patent an idea, you have to come up with a detailed drawing of your concept.

IDEAS

Invention Fail

PLASTIC BAGS

Although cheap, clever and useful, plastic bags became too popular for their own good and ended up as an environmental hazard; these days, reusable bags are preferred.

INVENTOR'S JOURNAL

Get yourself a nice, big notebook and use it to jot down ideas and sketches. Make sure you record the different stages of your invention's development and put a date next to each entry as well as a record of your progress. This could be useful if you have to prove that you really are the brains behind such a brilliant idea.

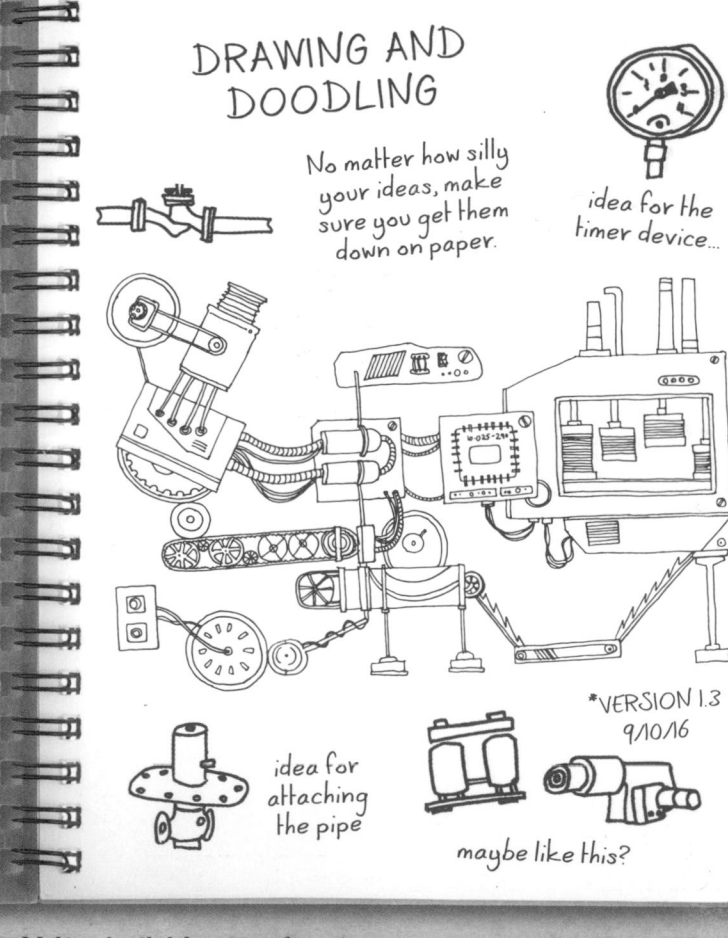

DRAWING AND DOODLING

No matter how silly your ideas, make sure you get them down on paper.

idea for the timer device...

*VERSION 1.3
9/10/16

idea for attaching the pipe

maybe like this?

Making detailed drawings of your invention ideas will help you to remember them.

THE 21ST-CENTURY JOURNAL

If you prefer to work on a computer or tablet, there's plenty of technology that can help. Check out Evernote, a great note-taking app that works on your smartphone, or online services like Pinterest, and the wonderfully-named Dribbble which let you collect and store inspiration from all over the Internet.

Online Research

Finding out how much raw materials are going to cost may not be as tough as you think, thanks to websites like Alibaba and Made In China. Here you'll be able to get estimates for millions of different components – everything from plastic sheeting and LED strip lights to inflatable items, electronics and much, much more.

Invention Win

SLAP BRACELET

Have you seen or worn a Slap Bracelet? This simple layered stainless steel band, coated with fabric or plastic starts out straight but then wraps itself snugly around your wrist when struck against it. It's incredibly simple, really cheap to make and has made its inventor – a teacher, by the way – a fortune.

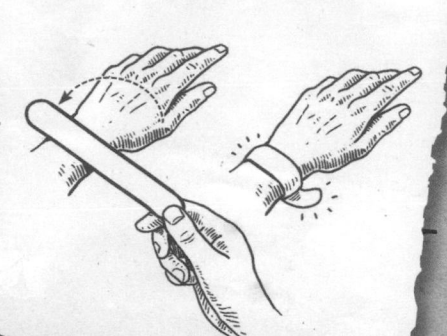

NUTS AND BOLTS

Even at this early stage, you need to start thinking practically about your invention. Here are some of the most important factors to consider and why they're important.

1. Who's going to make it? If you do it yourself it'll be cheaper; but maybe you could get your school involved – at least to help with the early versions.

2. What's it going to be made from? Can you also produce a test version using materials that are cheaper and easier to work with (modelling clay instead of welded metal for example, or inexpensive balsa wood instead of carbon-fibre)?

3. How long will each one take to make? If your invention is so complicated that it can't be mass-produced, then you may have to think again.

4. How much is it going to cost to make? You won't know precise costs at this stage but it's important to have a sense of how much the invention costs to make compared with how much you think you can sell it for.

GENIUS INVENTIONS

These inventions were so ahead of their time that it took years – sometimes thousands of years – for them to be recognised as the brilliant ideas they are.

1800BCE

THE FLUSHING TOILET

This marvel of ancient Greek engineering was in regular use around 1800BCE. Rainwater stored in tanks was released and – thanks to gravity – carried everything away with it through a system of underground clay pipes. Puzzlingly, the idea didn't catch on for another 3,000 years, when people got it into their heads that using a hole in the ground wasn't, you know, very civilized.

The first flushing toilet was invented thousands of years before purpose-made toilet paper. Try wiping that from your mind!

1400s

THE PARACHUTE

When Leonardo da Vinci designed the parachute way back in around 1485, it didn't catch on for one very good reason: flying hadn't been invented, so nobody needed a parachute. It wasn't until the late 1700s that parachutes were 'discovered' again and used by hot-air balloonists in times of emergency.

HELP!

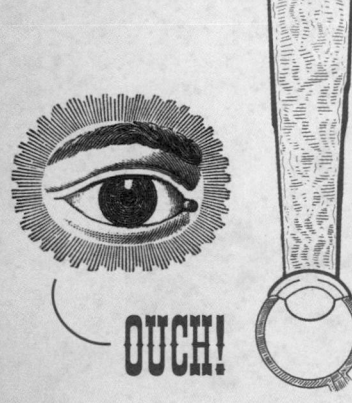

THE VENDING MACHINE

In the first century, people would swap gold coins for holy water, believing it could cure disease. Unfortunately, they'd often take too much, so an inventor called Hero came up with a device that weighed their coins and then gave them exactly the right amount of water. That's pretty much what happens when you buy a bar of chocolate from a vending machine today.

This diagram shows what Hero's machine would have looked like.

1636

CONTACT LENSES

In 1636, the French philosopher René Descartes came up with a way of helping people to see more clearly – he found that pressing a glass tube filled with water directly against your eye could magnify objects. Cumbersome and uncomfortable (you couldn't blink!), it was the forerunner of the contact lens.

OUCH!

1981

THE XEROX STAR

Think that Apple or Microsoft invented the modern computer with its icons, menus, windows and mouse? Think again. In 1981 Xerox Corp introduced the 8010 'Star' workstation which had all of those features already built in. Unfortunately, it had about the same memory as a pocket calculator and cost $20,000!

ONLY $20,000!

DESIGN IT!

OK, so you've come up with a great invention but, so far, you're the only one who knows what it looks like! The next step is to show other people, and for that you'll need a design.

1. PENCIL AT THE READY

The easiest way to produce a design is to draw it on paper with a pencil. At this stage it doesn't have to be an exact version of your invention, but it does need to show its main features and functions clearly so that anyone can see what it does at a glance. Produce several drawings on a single sheet of paper, each showing your invention from a different angle. If it has moving parts – such as doors that open and close – you should show these in action, too.

Don't worry if it takes a few attempts to get your drawing right.

Help, I can't draw!

There are plenty of inexpensive ways to help you produce a drawing that does your invention justice – even if you can't draw. Try some of these:

☞ Use plastic templates or stencils which have shapes already cut out to help you draw more accurately.

☞ Draw on a computer. Most programs include ways to smooth out shaky lines as well as adding fancy colour fills and shading to make drawings look professional.

☞ Take an art class or find video lessons online.

☞ Get a friend who's better at drawing to help you out (maybe for a cut of the profits if the invention's a success!).

2. WHAT'S IN A NAME?

Give your design a clear title and description – even at this early stage you need to be thinking about what it's going to be called and how you're going to sum up what it does in a few words.

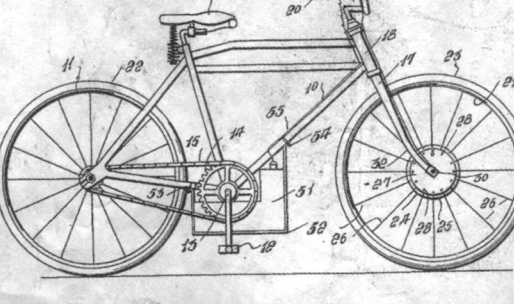

3. WHAT SIZE IS IT?

Finally, add a second, everyday object to the drawing – like a pencil or an apple – for scale so people can see how big your invention will be.

Silly, snappy or sensible: every invention needs a name. What other names can you think of to call a bicycle?

QUICK DRAW

If you're going to produce a design for your invention the old-fashioned way, then you'll need these tools of the trade.

GATHER YOUR KIT

Your invention drawing kit should consist of these 5 things: pencils (and a sharpener, of course), erasers, a ruler, graph paper and a compass.

1 Think all pencils are the same? Think again. There are 20 common 'grades' of pencil, from very hard and fine right through to ultra-soft and dark ones. We'd recommend a 2H pencil, which is fine enough to produce neat, even strokes without breaking all the time.

2 There are four main types of eraser: rubber, gum, kneaded and vinyl. Although ordinary rubber erasers are good for most jobs, if you're doing very fine work it's worth considering a vinyl eraser – especially a pencil vinyl eraser, which looks like a pencil and can be sharpened like one.

3 A clear plastic ruler is best for this kind of work.

2H HB 2B 6B

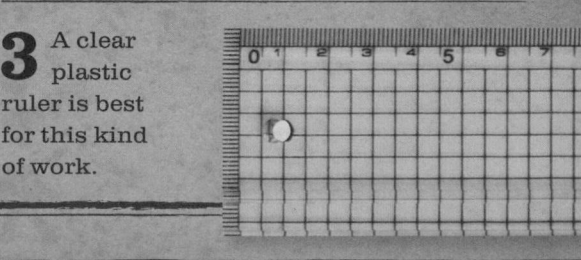

4 Graph paper is ordinary white paper divided up into hundreds of tiny squares. This not only makes it easier to draw horizontal and vertical lines but also angled lines because you can use the squares to position whatever you're drawing correctly. Acid-free paper is best because it won't fade too much if you leave it in the sun.

5 A compass is a precision instrument that helps you to draw perfect circles and arcs with pinpoint accuracy – elements that you'll find yourself drawing again and again in your designs.

THE INVENTOR'S 'OFFICE'

You'll need lots of natural light and, while you're probably not going to have access to a proper architect-style raised drawing board (yet!), you do need a good, flat, uncluttered surface to work on.

GET SMART

Remember that an invention can also exist in the digital world, rather than the physical one – so if you've got a great idea for a smartphone app, or a web service, you can use illustration software or even something like PowerPoint to demonstrate what it will look like and how it will work.

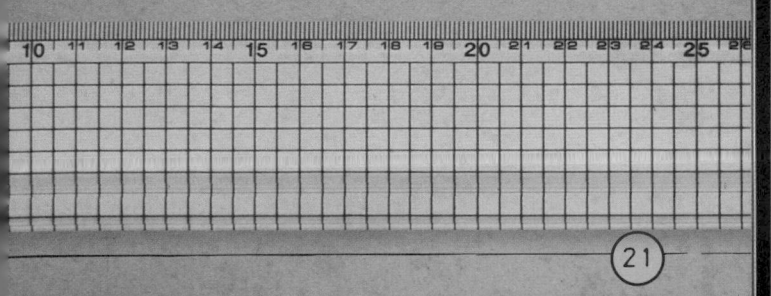

route *planner*

pick your mode of transport

WHAT'S A SCALE DRAWING?

Let's imagine you've invented the car. You want to draw your car design to show other people but in order to do that you'd need about 20 sheets of A4 just to reproduce the length! Obviously that's not practical, so instead you can do a scale drawing where you decide that a measurement on the piece of paper equals a different measurement in real life.

SHRINKING IN SIZE

It works like this. You decide that a centimetre on paper is the same as 20 centimetres in real life. This allows you to produce a small version of your design where all the different bits are the right size relative to each other. This particular scale would be written as 1/20, 1:20 or 1 to 20. If you make a design using this method, be sure to make the scale nice and clear so people don't get confused about the size of your invention.

SCALE= 1:20

CRAZY BUT TRUE

This bizarre 'pillow' completely envelopes your head and has a hole on each side for your hands so you can lay your head on the table in front of you and go to sleep. As some people have pointed out, it makes your head look like a giant bulb of garlic. (It does look comfy, though.)

OSTRICH
PILLOW

Wearing an ostrich pillow allows you to rest your head comfortably wherever you are.

If you blow up this drawing 20 times it should match the dimensions of a real car exactly.

Invention Win

ROLLER DRUM

In countries where drought is common, people often have to walk for miles, carrying heavy containers filled with water. As people can't carry much, this often means making many journeys over the course of the day. An invention called the Roller Drum consists of a drum with a hole right through the middle, through which you can thread a length of rope and pull the drum behind you as you walk. This is much easier than carrying a container and allows you to transport nearly five times as much water in one go.

BUILD IT!

The thinking part is now behind you and so it's time to get on with the practical stuff – the only way you'll discover whether or not your invention is truly ready for the wide world is by building it. So what are you waiting for?

THE PROTOTYPE

Before building the real thing, many inventors have a series of dummy runs, where they build something that looks like their invention in order to see whether people like it or not. This is known as a prototype and it is especially worth doing if the look and feel of the invention is important. Your prototype can be made out of pretty much anything – household items, stuff from a craft shop – because at this stage it's a bit like show-and-tell at school. You just want to give people an idea of what the final product will be like.

THE FIVE LAWS OF PROTOTYPING

☞ **1.** You must test and make improvements to the design of your invention.

☞ **2.** You must test the way that it works again when you use different materials to build it.

☞ **3.** When you put your invention under people's noses, they must be able to understand what it is.

☞ **4.** When others hold your invention in their hands, then poke it, prod it and even smell it, they shouldn't be able to say 'you'll never make it – it's just a pipe dream'.

☞ **5.** When Laws 1, 2, 3 and 4 have been followed, then Law 5 comes into effect: people will take you and your invention seriously.

TOTALLY POINTLESS!

Invention Fail

PIZZA SLICER FORK

The Pizza Slicer Fork – it's literally a fork with a tiny sharp cutting wheel attached, so you can cut your pizza into bite-sized pieces and eat it with only one hand. Fiddly and pointless.

EASY PROTOTYPING

Depending on what you're trying to build (and your budget), there are various good prototyping materials you can use. Here are some of our favourites.

PAPER AND CARD

Yes, you can make a prototype of your invention using ordinary paper and card. Paper is simple to cut, roll and fold, while card is easily cut and shaped. For both we'd recommend getting a craft board – a sturdy plastic board with grid lines that you can use to line up paper and card before cutting them with a craft knife. You can also use brass fasteners (sometimes called split pins) to create moving parts quickly and easily.

Take care when using sharp knives. Ask an adult to supervise or, better still, to cut objects out for you.

24 25 26 27 28 29 30 cm

Balsa is an ideal material for making model planes as it's very light.

BALSA WOOD

This is an incredibly lightweight wood that's been popular with model makers for many years. Balsa wood is easy to shape with a craft knife and ruler. It's also easy to glue together in layers to form complicated shapes and it's cheap – so if you make a mistake you can just recycle it and start again. It has other properties too that may be useful for your invention: it floats on water; it's incredibly light (making it good for anything that needs to be suspended or propelled through the air); it's good at retaining heat; it's flexible, so you can bend it around other objects and it's soft and easy to shape using sandpaper.

Perfect prototype?

Remember, your first prototype doesn't need to have exactly the same features as the finished invention. It's supposed to make you think about your invention and how it will eventually work.

Why is balsa wood so light?

A growing balsa tree is around 60 per cent water, so when the trees are cut down, they must be dried in a special oven – called a kiln – in order to remove all that moisture. That's why the finished wood is so light.

ADVANCED PROTOTYPING

Once you've made a simple prototype and have an idea of what your invention will look like, it's time to raise the stakes a little by making something more advanced.

MOULDABLE PLASTIC

This sounds a bit specialized, but it isn't really. There are two main types. The first are little pellets that need to be heated up (usually by dropping them into hot water). This turns them into globs of see-through glue that you can shape. The second type is like soft putty which you can mould straight out of the packet, but which keeps its shape when left at room temperature.

Both types of mouldable plastic are great for creating all sorts of shapes, sticking parts of your invention to other parts and acting as shock absorbers. They keep their shape but stay flexible and some have a super-smooth finish which means they can be used to make rotating joints.

Mouldable plastic is great for shaping into anything you want. If you don't like what you've done, you can simply heat it up again and re-shape it until you get it right.

Invention Win

MULTI-PURPOSE CABLE CLIPS

These little 'drops' of silicon have a groove through the middle that grips cables securely. Incredibly cheap, they can be used anywhere and were probably prototyped using mouldable plastic.

Household junk

Keep an eye out for everyday objects lying around the house – items like screws, nuts and bolts from the family toolbox, elastic bands, the bristles from an old scrubbing brush, paperclips, string, or even empty coffee tins. The missing component you're looking for could be staring you in the face.

OFF THE SHELF

If you don't feel confident enough to try your hand at making a prototype from scratch, you may be able to use objects and items that already exist. Here are some good sources for these 'off-the-shelf' components.

1 **Your old toy box.** Here you'll find all manner of items that can be used in your prototype – wheels, axles, old model cars, plane and train bodies, bits of plastic and lots more.

2 **Construction kits.** These can include plastic building blocks and metal construction kits, as well as specialist systems that are aimed at serious creators and inventors (but these can be quite expensive).

3 **Hardware and DIY shops.** Here you'll find all kinds of items you can use, especially in the plumbing and electrical departments. Look for plastic pipes, funnels, U-bends, wiring and so on. A lot of this stuff can be fitted together without using tools.

ESSENTIAL INVENTIONS

Some inventions are so useful that it's hard to imagine everyday life without them. Here are five couldn't-do-without-them inventions.

The teeth in a zip mesh tightly together as they pass through the slider.

1913

THE ZIP

Since its invention at the end of 1913, the zip has become an indispensable part of modern life. Easier and quicker than buttons, this brilliantly simple device uses a mechanical slider to pull two sets of 'teeth' together. Zips can be made of metal, plastic or polyester and are so efficient they're used on space suits!

1844

THE MATCH

Matches had been around for hundreds of years before Gustav Erik Pasch invented the 'safety match' in 1844. Previous attempts had been dangerous and poisonous (the scrapings from a single packet were enough to kill someone). Pasch's innovation was to separate the two ingredients that reacted with each other to light the match: one went on the side of the box, the other on the match head. Hundreds of millions of matches are struck every year.

1973
GLOBAL POSITIONING SYSTEM

The Global Positioning System (GPS) – 24 satellites orbiting the Earth – started life as a project for the US military but is now used to help car drivers find where they're going, by athletes and cyclists who want to measure performance and by social media sites to add location data to your posts.

1901
THE SAFETY RAZOR

Before the disposable razor was invented in 1901, people would use a cut-throat razor to shave. As the name suggests, these razors were not designed with safety in mind. Disposable razors on the other hand, were encased in a sheath, which made it more difficult to cut the skin accidentally. They also helped invent a new style of marketing – inventor King Camp Gillette sold the razor cheaply but made the replacement blades quite expensive. Genius!

SPLENDID!

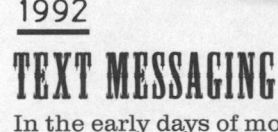

I've just thought up a really cool new invention.

Great! Send me a pic of your design

1992
TEXT MESSAGING

In the early days of mobile phones, the network was idle when people weren't actually making calls, so companies came up with the idea of using this spare capacity to send and receive short messages – what we call 'texts'. Although they were invented almost as an afterthought, by 2010, the phone networks were sending 6.1 trillion texts a year!

TEST IT!

Now you've got a working model, it's time to see how your invention behaves in the real world. This can be a really tough time, because you'll discover that not everyone understands what you're trying to do. It is, however, an important part of the process.

WHAT DO YOU MEAN, YOU DON'T KNOW WHAT IT DOES?!

When you've spent weeks (or even months) working on an invention, you know it so well that everything about it seems obvious: push this and that happens, turn this and it does that. So it's very important to give it to a selection of people who've never seen it before and who don't know anything about it. This will help you to understand whether your invention – at least in its current form – is going to work or not.

Testing Times

Here are the basic questions you need to ask, and the three different ways to ask them.

<u>Give</u> your invention to the test subject and see what happens.

- ☛ Are they holding it correctly?
- ☛ Do they understand what it does?
- ☛ Can they make it work?
- ☛ Can they make it work easily?
- ☛ What do they think of it?

<u>Tell</u> them what the invention does and then ask the questions again.

<u>Show</u> them what the invention does and then ask the same questions. They will let you see if people have any problems using your invention, even after they've been shown how it works.

Leave the room

When companies test a product, they'll often sit behind a one-way mirror so they can watch as would-be customers try to use it. This is because people behave differently if they know that the inventor is observing them. Since you can't afford a one-way mirror, you can get someone else to film the testing process with a camera phone so you can watch it later.

GIVE IT A GO

Sometimes people need a little bit more encouragement and guidance to understand your invention, so it might be worthwhile giving a practical demonstration. In the 1850s, American inventor Elisha Otis developed a safety elevator which would come to a halt if its hoisting rope snapped. Uptake was slow, so he arranged a demonstration at the New York World's Fair in 1854. The show was a success and sales soared.

Otis demonstrates his invention in front of a cheering crowd.

Pictured in 1900, the inventor Nikola Tesla calmly tests his latest invention – a machine for transmitting huge bolts of electricity!

REAL-WORLD RULES

One of the most effective ways to test an invention is to get people to use it in different situations. This helps you to discover lots of important information about your invention. Here are some real-world rules to apply.

8 REAL-WORLD RULES

• Does it break easily or is it durable? If your invention is too flimsy, people will complain.

• Can it be used outside as well as inside? For example, if it has a screen, can you read it in sunlight?

• If it's designed to be portable, is it light enough and small enough to be carried around easily?

• Does it need a lot of space to be used comfortably and will this prevent it from being used in a crowded place, such as a train?

• Does it work the same every time, or is there a knack to making it work properly?

• If it uses batteries, how long do they last?

• If it's an invention that's supposed to be used outside in cold weather, can you make it work while wearing gloves?

• Can it be used with your eyes closed, or in the dark?

Be consistent

When you're testing your invention on different people, make sure you ask them all the same questions (see page 32). Gathering data in an organised way like this helps you analyse how your invention could be improved upon. For example, if eight out of ten people think it weighs too much, then it's probably too heavy.

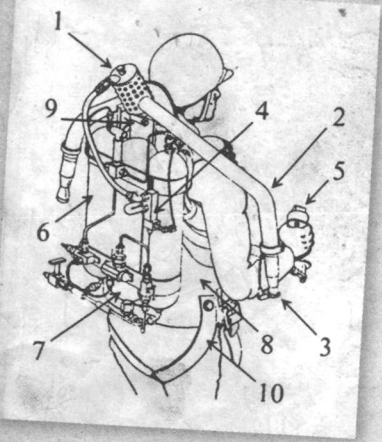

INVENTION FAILS

Over the centuries, there have probably been more invention failures than successes. Here are four inventions that fell at the first hurdle.

1 Invented in 1964, the phone answering robot picked up the phone but didn't have a voice and couldn't record or play back messages. Plus it looked terrifying.

2 The Bell Rocket Belt took off in 1961 – 21 seconds after take-off, it ran out of fuel.

3 The Advanced Passenger Train developed in the 1970s had a tilting mechanism to help it corner at super-high speeds. Sadly, the motion made everyone on board feel horribly sick. Improvements in the mechanism mean that some of the latest trains can now tilt as they corner without causing sickness.

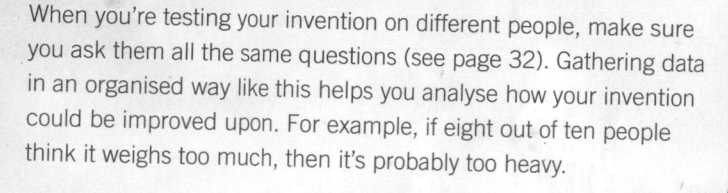

4 In 1628, the *Vasa*, the world's most revolutionary warship, slipped her moorings in front of a cheering crowd, and then promptly sank.

U IS FOR USABILITY

If your invention is an app for a tablet, smartphone or web service, then you can do what's called a usability study. This sounds complicated, but isn't.

CREATING TASKS

Let's say your app is designed to let people put fancy coloured filters over photos they've snapped on their phone (don't invent this – it's been done loads of times). What you would do is create a task for the tester that goes like this:

1. Take a photo
2. Find a filter you like
3. Apply the filter to the photograph
4. Save the new photograph
5. Upload it to a social media site

Notice that these are not instructions – you're telling the tester what you'd like them to do, rather than explaining how they should do it.

How many versions of the same photo can you make?

Recording

If you search for 'screen recorder', you'll find plenty of apps that will record the screen of a phone, tablet or computer. This way, you can watch testers using your product to see which bits they find easy and which bits are difficult. Some apps can even use the device's camera to record testers' facial expressions.

KEEP GOING

It's said that Thomas Edison tried 1,000 times to invent the light bulb before he was successful. He famously refused to acknowledge these experiments as failures but instead said that the successful light bulb took 1,000 steps to invent.

Edison was a great believer in 'If at first you don't succeed, try, try, try, try, try and try again' (with a few more tries after that!).

Invention Fail

THE BABY CAGE

In the 1930s in London's fashionable borough Chelsea, families who didn't have gardens still wanted their babies to get plenty of healthy, fresh air – so they hung them out of the window in cages. The idea didn't catch on.

What could possibly be wrong with putting a baby in a cage high above the streets of a busy city?!

Invention Win

TOP-DOWN SQUEEZE BOTTLE

Beautifully simple, this is a clever valve, which opens when the bottle is squeezed and closes when the pressure is released. The idea works for sauces, shampoo and all sorts of other things. The inventor Paul Brown eventually sold his company for $14 million.

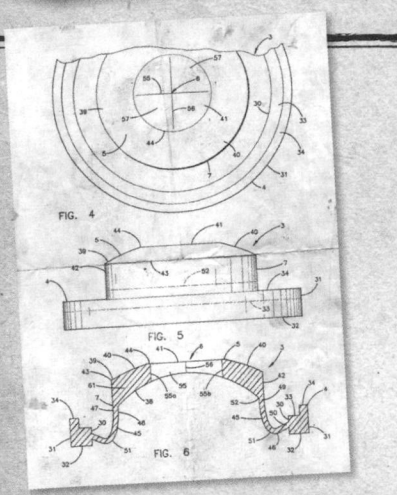

FIG. 4

FIG. 5

FIG. 6

IMPROVE IT!

Having shown your invention to different people, you'll need to analyse their feedback and then decide whether or not to make some changes to the design based on what they have said.

BE ANALYTICAL

If you tested your invention on eight people and asked them the same five questions (see pages 32–33), then you can make a table with the questions down one side and the people's names along the top. Complete the table with the answers they gave you and you'll be able to see at a glance where the main issues are with your invention. Those are the ones you need to fix.

	Name	Name	Name	Name	Name	Name	Name	Name
Are they holding it correctly?								
Do they understand what it does?								
Can they make it work?								
Can they make it work easily?								
What do they think of it?								

Danger!

Perhaps your invention has a sharp edge, gets hot after too much use or perhaps it has a nasty smell. If the tests from the previous chapter reveal that your invention has safety issues, then you may need to add an 'advisory' label. It doesn't mean the invention is unsafe, but it does mean that users should follow certain guidelines.

SMALLER, LIGHTER, STRONGER, BETTER

1. Is It Too Heavy?
Consider switching to a lighter material (aluminium is lighter than steel, for example); can parts of the invention be made hollow instead of solid or can you drill holes in it to lighten the load?

2. Is It Too Big?
Can you make your invention smaller by just scaling down the size of the components?

Alternatively, if it uses handles, knobs, buttons, catches or other controls, can they be made smaller or placed more conveniently?

3. Is It Too Flimsy?
Can you replace parts of the invention that are likely to break with stronger ones? Perhaps you can use see-through plastic instead of glass, or bamboo instead of balsa?

Invention Win

THE CAT'S EYE
In 1933, Percy Shaw was driving home in the dark when the headlights of his car were reflected back in the eyes of a cat. This inspired him to invent the little reflective flexible domes that run along the centre of a road and help keep cars on the correct side at night.

Even a great invention can be improved. Over time, phones have become smaller, easier to operate and able to carry out more tasks.

SETTING INSTRUCTIONS

If it turns out your invention isn't quite as easy to understand and use as you thought it was, you might need to write some instructions – a manual. The best way is to write a series of numbered step-by-step instructions that explain how to use the invention as intended.

READ THE MANUAL!

For example, imagine you've invented a way to feed your dog at a specific time of day. The instructions might go like this:

1. Open the lid of the feeder.

2. If the feeder has been used before, remove the inner bowl and empty any leftovers into the bin.

3. Wipe the inner bowl with a damp cloth and put it back in the feeder.

4. Fill to the line around the rim with dry dog food.

5. Close the lid.

6. Adjust the timer on the back of the feeder by turning it to the correct time of day.

7. Get on with your day and don't worry about the dog going hungry!

FAQs

Depending on feedback, you could also include a separate page called *Troubleshooting* or *FAQs* – which stands for 'Frequently Asked Questions'. This might include problems like:

1. Help, my feeder is smelly!

2. The feeder won't close.

3. Do I need to dry the inner bowl after wiping?

4. How much food should I leave for a small dog?

After each one, write a short answer that helps someone solve the problem.

Record a video

If you're more of a visual person, you can always get someone to record a video of you using your invention, so that other people can see how it works.

Invention Fail

THE PARACHUTE JACKET

Franz Reichelt developed a coat with large flaps which he was convinced would slow any fall, allowing the wearer to float safely to the ground. In 1912, he decided to test his invention by jumping off the Eiffel Tower in Paris. He plummeted to his death, leaving a 15-centimetre-deep hole in the ground where he fell. Hundreds of people watched the tragedy unfold and it was even recorded on camera.

While Reichelt's parachute jacket failed, its influence can be seen in the flying suits used successfully today.

TERRIBLE INVENTIONS

We're not talking about failed inventions here – there are probably millions of those – but actual real inventions that went sour, sometimes with catastrophic results.

1937

HYDROGEN BLIMPS

A blimp is a huge flying balloon big enough to carry people, and the obvious choice to keep it in the air is helium – the second lightest element in the universe. However, helium is expensive, so balloon designers turned to hydrogen to keep their blimps flying. Unfortunately, hydrogen is one of the most flammable elements in the universe, which spelled disaster in 1937, when the *Hindenburg* caught fire and crashed to the ground in just 36 seconds.

The Hindenburg, *then the longest airship in the world, burst into flames after completing its first transatlantic crossing.*

LAAA!

1997

AUTO-TUNE

Auto-tune means that even terrible singers can make records. Out-of-tune notes can be corrected on a computer – just like spelling mistakes in a word processed document – to make a singer's performance always sound perfect. It can even be used live in concert and frankly, feels like cheating.

This is what asbestos looks like in its natural state.

1973
THE FLYING CAR

Yes, it's a car and a small plane stuck together. There's not even any real attempt to 'smooth' the join either – it looks like someone took the cabin off a plane and stuck a car in its place. Even worse is that the car is a Ford Pinto, which became notorious for its tendency to explode (yes, explode) if another vehicle drove into the back of it.

1900s
ASBESTOS FIREPROOFING

Used for fireproofing buildings until the late 1970s, this natural material (made from billions of microscopic fibres) is strong and resists heat well. Unfortunately, those same fibres are so small (much smaller than a human hair) that they can be inhaled easily and cause terrible damage to the lungs and airways. It is no longer used as a building material and any existing asbestos has to be removed very carefully.

WARNING: MAY EXPLODE!

PHEW!

Strangely, the helicopter ejector seat hasn't caught on. The Kamov KA is one of the only models to use it.

1982
THE HELICOPTER EJECTOR SEAT

Think about it. Dismissed by most sensible people as the craziest safety feature ever, this invention is actually used in the Russian-built Kamov KA helicopter series. The trick is to make sure the pilot blows off the helicopter blades before employing the ejector seat. Otherwise...

PATENT IT!

Before you start making your invention you may want to stop people from copying it. It's not essential, but if you're serious about your invention, a patent will protect it from copycats.

HOW DO I PROTECT MY INVENTION?

The best way is to apply for a patent. This is a legal document that gives you the sole right to make, use, import and sell your invention for 20 years; though you'll have to renew the patent every year so that it stays in effect. This means that if someone else tries to steal your idea, you can stop them – and the law will be on your side. Keep in mind that if you get a patent in the UK, it only applies to the UK and not anywhere else in the world.

The patent drawing for a bathtub that rocks back and forth – no, we don't know what the point of it is either!

YOU CAN FIND THE EUROPEAN PATENT OFFICE AT: WWW.EPO.ORG/INDEX.HTML

What kind of invention can I patent?

The rules say that your invention must be:

☞ New
☞ Something that can be made or used
☞ A genuine invention, rather than a modification of something that already exists

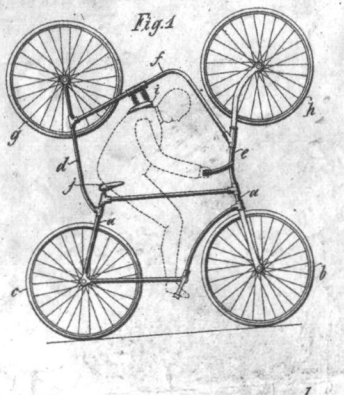

Fig.1

Fig.2

Want to loop-the-loop?
Then this is the bicycle for you!

HOW DO I GET A PATENT?

As we said back on page 13, the first thing to do is make sure someone else hasn't already taken out a patent on an invention that's similar to yours. The good news is that there's a website that lets you search the patents registered in more than 90 countries from all over the world. The bad news is that the site (and the language used) is difficult to understand and to navigate. You may need to enlist the help of a friendly adult at this point.

SEARCHING...

How long does it take?

If you're hoping to have your application for a patent granted in a few days, you're in for a shock. Most successful ones take anywhere between three and five years!

HOW MUCH DOES ALL THIS COST?

This is the sticking point for many would-be inventors. The office in charge of looking after patents in the UK admits that filing for a patent is 'complicated' and says that only one inventor in 20 is able to complete the process on their own. If you get professional help, it's likely to cost around £4,000!

FIVE INVENTORS WHO DIDN'T PATENT THEIR INVENTIONS

1 **Douglas Engelbart** – invented the computer mouse way back in 1968 but let the patent expire.

The very first mouse was surrounded by a wooden casing.

2 **Geoffrey Dummer** – everyone ignored his microchip concept, then US tech company Texas Instruments patented it six years later and the modern computer industry was born.

Geoffrey Dummer

3 **Daisuke Inoue** – invented the karaoke machine, which went on to become one of the most popular entertainment devices of modern times. (Incidentally, 'karaoke' is Japanese for 'empty orchestra'.)

4 **Sir Tim Berners-Lee** – yes, the man who invented the World Wide Web – didn't apply for a patent because he believed it should be freely available for everyone to use. So at least he did it deliberately!

Sir Tim Berners-Lee – inventor of the World Wide Web.

5 **Alexey Pajitnov** – invented the computer game *Tetris*, where building blocks fall from the top of the screen and must be arranged to slot into the empty spaces below. Sadly he was working in the Soviet Union at the time – so the Communist state owned his invention!

Invention Fail

THE BABY MOP

It's a onesie with little strips of mop sewn into the arms and legs. As the baby crawls along, the mop cleans the floor! Is it a joke, or for real? You decide!

CLEANS AS HE CRAWLS!

Invention Win

THE WALKMAN

Although it seems dated now, the Sony Walkman (a portable music player that let you listen to audio cassette tapes on the move) was the precursor for every battery-powered mobile device we use today. It's now nearly 40 years old.

PRODUCE IT!

So you've crossed the Ts and dotted the Is and are happy that your invention is ready to be manufactured. Here are a few ideas to get the production line rolling.

THE FACTORY FLOOR

A modern factory is a hive of activity where hundreds (and sometimes thousands) of people and robots work. Each person or robot carries out a particular task, taking the product one step nearer to completion as it moves along a production line. Follow these steps to create your own 'factory floor'.

1 **Light and power.** Chances are that you'll need electricity – even if it's just light so that you can see what you're doing. Remember that you may be working on this after school when it's starting to get dark.

2 **Dedicated areas for each stage.** Most inventions will require several steps to make or assemble, so you may need different areas, such as a clear space for folding or cutting or a well-lit area with a magnifying glass for close-up work. You could also add corkboards above each area with simple instructions to remind you what goes where.

light

paper
cutter

light

corkboard

desk space

magnifying
glass

prototype
of invention

Find a club or society to help

There's a lot of interest in inventions at the moment and a number of 'Inventor Clubs' dedicated to helping people like you make their dreams come true. Your best bet is to search for Inventor Clubs in your area on the Internet. Many are associated with universities and colleges and some have really good facilities. It's also worth looking for online sites like 'Quirky.com', which are designed to partner with inventors and help them make their ideas a reality.

Henry Ford and mass production

The man behind the Ford motor car is credited with promoting the production line. Instead of building one vehicle at a time from start to finish, he came up with the idea of a moving production line with 'stations' where different parts would be added (electrics, wheels, doors and so on). The bare-bones chassis was loaded at one end and the finished car came out the other. It revolutionised production and resulted in the first truly affordable car – the Ford Model T.

3 **Storage units on wheels with sliding drawers** and see-through fronts so you can see what's inside. These will also provide extra work surfaces and will keep your various tools, components and other invention-related items organised where you can find them easily.

4 **If your invention needs to 'rest'** between stages (perhaps so something can dry or harden) then you should create separate areas where you can store it safely while you get on with something else.

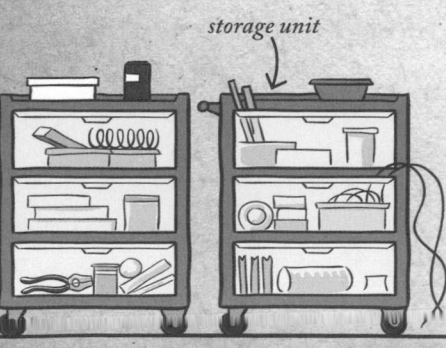

storage unit

drying area

fan

plans chest

SAFETY FIRST

Here are some simple rules to keep you safe in your 'factory'. Make sure you get an adult to help you.

READ THIS FIRST

There's an old saying: 'Your mind is sharper than any knife.' When you're working with hand or power tools, needles, craft knives – anything that can cut you – just think about what you're about to do before you do it. This is the best way to avoid accidents and to stay safe.

1 Avoid shorts and flip-flops. Wear sensible clothing and tough shoes – especially if your invention is heavy.

2 Wear safety goggles and gloves if you're handling chemicals or hot objects; wear a mask if making your invention creates smoke or dust.

3 Got long hair? Tie it back.

4 If you're using glue, make sure that your 'factory' is well ventilated (open a window or two).

KEEP A FIRST-AID KIT STOCKED AND HANDY – YOU NEVER KNOW WHEN AN ACCIDENT MIGHT HAPPEN.

After school

It may be worth talking to your teachers in the science, design and technology departments to see if they run an after school class that might be helpful for building your invention. If not, ask them for their help to start one.

Get organised

If your invention uses eight different components, store them separately so that you don't need to root around for the next one. This also helps you to see when you're running low on a particular item.

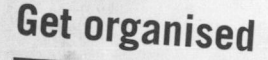

5 Don't work when you're tired – this is when you're most likely to make a mistake or have an accident.

6 When you finish, always tidy up so that your 'factory' is ready for action the following day.

7 If you're working in a shed or garage, make sure you lock your workspace and secure any valuable or dangerous components away from inquisitive friends and siblings.

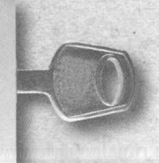

8 Hopefully you won't need a fire extinguisher, but you should always make sure you have one to hand just in case!

3-D PRINTING

Some inventions are just too difficult to produce on your own. You may need to invest in items that you don't already have, such as tools, components and materials, they may require more space than you have at home, or the process may be too noisy or too smelly.

THE D-I-Y FUTURE

3-D printers produce three-dimensional objects using a combination of nylon and resin. They use a digital model of your invention and take instructions from this to 'print' the object by building it up one thin layer at a time. Since they were invented, they have become more affordable and readily available. You might even be able to find one in your school.

There are now 3-D printers that are small and cheap enough to own in the home. These would let any would-be inventor construct their own prototypes and products, without having to rely on someone else.

Many plastic 3-D printers use filaments of plastic that are fed through on a spool.

Invention Win

3-D PRINTING

The ability to print out three-dimensional objects is a complete game-changer and will revolutionise the way inventors design and create special components. As more materials become available, the range of items you'll be able to print will expand. There are even 3-D printers that can produce the parts to make other 3-D printers!

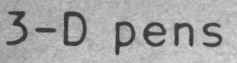
3-D pens

If you want to create a quick model of your design, then a 3-D pen could be the answer. This lets you draw solid 3-D shapes using 'threads' of plastic ink!

This model of an aircraft was made using a 3-D pen.

LICENSING

If building the model yourself is too problematic, then you can always license your invention to someone else. A licence is a legally binding agreement that lets someone else manufacture and sell the invention in return for either a one-off fee or a percentage (called a royalty) of each one they can sell. Licensing deals usually last for a specific amount of time, such as three years, after which control of the invention will return to you.

3-D PRINTERS CAN PRODUCE OBJECTS USING METAL, PAPER, CERAMICS AND RUBBER. THERE ARE ALSO PLANS TO PRODUCE 3-D PRINTERS THAT PRINT WITH FOOD!

HILARIOUS INVENTIONS

Some inventions are so whacky, so off-the-wall and so unlikely that they're almost too hilarious for words. Almost. Here are five of the funniest.

2007

THE HAMSTER-POWERED PAPER SHREDDER

We're not convinced you can buy one – yet – but this is too good not to mention. Insert paper in the top and when the hamster runs around the wheel inside the cage, the paper is drawn through the blades and shredded. This then makes a soft bed for 'Hammy' at the bottom of the cage. Pure genius.

1939

THE GOOFYBIKE

Built in 1939, the creation of Charles Steinlauf was designed to carry his entire family. The bike is not just a miracle of over-engineering (the Goofybike is so cumbersome that it has to be controlled with a car steering wheel), but it's also a symbol of 1930s sexism – note that dad and son pedal and steer, while mum sews and the daughter just sits there.

1999

THE ANIMAL TOY

This patent was granted in the United States. 'An apparatus for use as a toy by an animal, for example a dog, to either fetch, carry or chew, includes a main section with at least one protrusion... that resembles a branch in appearance... Various textured surfaces including camouflage colourings are anticipated as are straight or curved main sections.' Yes, it's a stick.

NO MORE ROLLING!

1978

THE EGG CUBER

Apparently, the roundness of eggs has been an unsolved problem for many years, resulting in corners not covered inside sandwiches and eggs rolling around on plates inconveniently. Enter the Egg Cuber. Take a hard-boiled egg and pop it in the cuber. Screw down the top and place in the fridge to get nice and cold. Remove, unscrew top and shake out your newly squared egg. Phew, what a relief.

2000s

THE FLYING ALARM CLOCK

It's an alarm clock with a propeller on the top. When this alarm sounds the propeller shoots into the air and glides round your room before coming to rest. The alarm on the clock continues until you get up, find the propeller and pop it back into the clock.

PACKAGE IT!

Before any great invention goes on sale, there's one last stage – you need to promote and package it attractively. Packaging serves two purposes. First, it explains the benefits of your invention clearly so that people understand what it does immediately; and second, it makes the invention look desirable.

IN THE SHOPS

Before you start, think about how your invention will be sold.

1 If it needs to sit on shelves in a shop, then the packaging will need to stack easily.

2 If it has a button which makes a noise when pushed, then it's worth making that accessible so customers can try it out, even when it's inside the packaging.

3 If you're going to sell it online or by mail order, then lighter packaging will reduce postage costs.

DOES YOUR PACKAGING MAKE YOUR INVENTION STAND OUT FROM THE CROWD?

Cardboard isn't just cardboard

Although cardboard is the most popular form of packaging by far, remember that there are many different kinds. A box that you get from Amazon for example, feels very different from one you get from Apple. The first is rough and practical – it does a job – while the second is smooth and feels luxurious. If you want to charge a premium price for your invention, then you'd better use premium packaging.

A sleek invention needs sleek packaging.

4 If people need to see the invention, then the box will need a plastic 'window' so customers can look inside.

5 You might also consider gimmick packaging, such as a completely plain box with the invention's name in tiny letters; or maybe just a logo with no name at all.

RIGHT MESSAGE?

Out of their bottles, some cleaning products may look like delicious soft drinks. If a product could be harmful, then it needs to carry warning messages and its packaging should be designed so that it doesn't look like it's meant to be drunk! Make sure your packaging suits your product.

PRACTICAL PACKAGING

While you can design your own box from scratch, there are some really useful websites that can help make the job easier. They provide step-by-step instructions for creating packaging that matches your needs exactly.

HELPING HANDS

If making a box sounds like too much work, search the Internet for 'gift packaging' and you'll find plenty of sites that sell fancy boxes in all shapes and sizes. Other websites take things a stage further and allow you to specify packaging accessories, linings and inserts. These elements may make your invention more secure when posting or more attractive when it's on the shelf – or they may just make it feel nicer when a customer opens the box.

The choice of packaging options is endless.

Good Photography

A modern camera phone will take photos that are good enough to use on packaging. You can also use these photos online when you come to promote your invention using blogs, websites and social media. Either shoot against a plain background or photograph the invention in context – for example, in the kitchen for a kitchen gadget or outside for a garden gadget.

Express Yourself

When promoting your invention, try to keep the message short and to the point. You need to focus on what your invention does, how it can benefit people and why they're going to love it. So if your invention is a set-top box that makes watching and recording your favourite TV programmes easier to organise, avoid saying something general, such as: 'The most amazing entertainment invention of all time'. Instead, make it more specific, such as the slogans shown here.

WATCHING TV WILL NEVER BE THE SAME AGAIN

THE SMARTER WAY TO WATCH YOUR TV

THIS SIMPLE GADGET WILL TRANSFORM YOUR TV EXPERIENCE FOREVER!

ADVERTISE AND PROMOTE

You might have the best invention in the world, but if nobody has heard about it then nobody's going to buy it – you need to spread the word.

WONDER SHOE

SPREAD THE MESSAGE

Here are some of the places you can promote your invention:

1 Your school
From noticeboards to science fairs to after school clubs, there are plenty of marketing opportunities here; you can also offer 20 per cent off the purchase price to kids from your own school.

2 Local newspapers and radio
Find the ones that cover your area and offer them an interview; local press love the whole 'young go-getter' thing.

CHECK WITH AN ADULT WHEN ACCESSING CERTAIN SOCIAL MEDIA SITES AS MANY OF THEM HAVE AGE RESTRICTIONS.

3 Your local area
Reach customers with a simple leaflet that you can design and print at home, and post through local letterboxes.

4 Social media
It costs nothing to set up a social media account and you may already have a ready-made network of family and friends you can sell to. Think about who might buy your invention and pick a social media outlet that targets them best.

5 **A website or blog**
There are plenty of services that let you set up a website or blog for free. You can then show off your invention, give hints and tips on how to use it and add video tutorials and testimonials from happy customers and so on; you can even set up an online shop and take orders!

Just Your Type

Any old font (sometimes called a typeface) won't do. Fonts can be used to help carry a message about your invention and there are some fonts that look good and work well together, while others can clash and create a confusing result. Along with colours, fonts can help to link all aspects of your invention, from packaging and advertising to marketing material and your website.

Helvetica — Sans serif fonts: clear and modern. Good for instructions and warnings.

Art Brush — Handwriting fonts: informal and young. Good for fun items and adverts.

Garamond — Serif fonts: traditional and serious. Good for creating a serious impression.

TRUE COLOURS

You may think that having lots of different colours will make your advertising, marketing and packaging stand out, but it's more likely to make it look like a mess. Designers use something called a 'colour palette', where they stick to just two, three or five colours (see below). Everything to do with your product should just use your chosen colour palette – and nothing else. There are plenty of websites that will generate a colour palette for you.

Analogous colours are next to each other.

Primary **YELLOW**

Secondary **GREEN**

Secondary **ORANGE**

Complementary colours are opposite each other.

Primary **BLUE**

Primary **RED**

Secondary **PURPLE**

Complementary   *Complementary plus black*

Split Complementary plus white and black

A colour wheel shows you how colours relate to each other. There are three primary colours – red, blue and yellow. Opposite these on the wheel are the secondary colours, which go well with the primaries – they are also known as complementary colours. Split complementary colours are found on either side of the complementary colours, and they can also work well with the primary colours.

IT'S A WRAP!

So that's it. We're done. Your invention is flying off the shelves, your bank account is bulging and you're recognised widely as the most successful young inventor of modern times. Congratulations. There's nothing more to be done except to wake up... come on, wake up sleepyhead, time get up and start inventing!

WHAT WE'VE LEARNED

1 That the invention process is a funny old thing – a combination of hard work (really hard work, sometimes) and bright ideas.

2 That in order to succeed, you have to be prepared to fail.

3 That the idea may come to you in a flash – a nanosecond – but turning it into reality could take months or even years.

4 That the whole process is incredibly rewarding – beyond any money you might make out of it.

5 That you'll need to master many different skills along the way: visionary, product designer, good communicator, product tester, safety officer, graphic designer, 'factory' worker, writer and product marketer.

> 'TO INVENT, YOU NEED A GOOD IMAGINATION AND A PILE OF JUNK.'
>
> Thomas Edison

THE HARD FACTS

I If at first you don't succeed, come up with a better idea!

N No-one is born to be an inventor; inventors invent themselves.

V Very few inventions ever see the light of day.

E Everyone has at least one great invention idea inside them.

N Never take 'no' for an answer; if you hit a problem or a setback, find a way round it.

T Truly great inventions are 1% inspiration and 99% perspiration.

IF YOU DON'T BELIEVE IN YOURSELF, YOU MAKE IT HARDER FOR OTHERS TO BELIEVE IN YOU.

AND FINALLY...

If you've made it this far, well done. You've shown that you've got the staying power to stick to your task, and we're sure that the lessons you've learned in these pages will help and inspire you as you continue to 'Invent it!' (whatever *it* turns out to be...).

INDEX